# How to Make Money Fast

# For Kids

**Entrepreneur Series**
**M. Usman**

**Mendon Cottage Books**

*JD-Biz Publishing*

### Our books are available at

1. Amazon.com
2. Barnes and Noble
3. Itunes
4. Kobo
5. Smashwords
6. Google Play Books

# Table of Contents

# Preface

It does not matter what your age is as we all need money. You can use it to buy just about anything you want in life. Unfortunately, many kids do not know how to make money. So they depend on their parents.

But who wants to ask for money from them all the time?

Even though you are a kid, you can make some money on your own. This may be to become more independent or to simply increase your income. Unfortunately, there is not much info on how you can get started with this.

But don't lose hope. In this book, I will show you some of the ways you can use to make money.

The best part with the methods in this book is that they are easy to understand. Additionally, they do not need extensive experience for you to get started. And since you may also be low on cash, these methods do not require huge investments.

Still, there is no substitution for hard work. If you are not willing to give these methods enough effort, you will not make a lot of money.
I wish you luck in your money-making endeavors. Enjoy the reading!

# Chapter 1: Clean People's Homes

Not only is a dirty house an embarrassment, but it can also harbor harmful animals and diseases. Current lifestyles don't offer many homeowners enough time clean their homes. For someone looking to make a quick buck, this is an opportunity to not miss.

House cleaning jobs don't require extensive experience. But even if you were to need it, you would become a master in less than a month.

Adding to that, tools you need to get started are readily available and cheap. This keeps start-up costs lower.

**What You Need**

Homeowners have different preferences on what you can use in cleaning their houses. So in most cases, you will not need to buy your own cleaning equipment; the owner will provide.

But that doesn't mean should not invest in the basics. Here is a list of things you will need:

- scrubby sponge

- toilet brush

- buckets

- microfiber mop

- rubber gloves

- extendable duster

- microfiber cloth.

Apart from the equipment, you will also need one other important thing – honesty. Would you open your house to someone who is not trustworthy? I bet you wouldn't. The same is true with the people you will be working for.

Another thing you shouldn't underestimate in this business is your fitness. You will spend a good part of the day standing (which can be a good thing if you don't work out much).

## Let People Know What You Do

When new in this business, getting clients isn't easy. Nobody knows what you do which makes it impossible to get in touch with you.

Since you are just a kid, other forms of advertising, like newspaper or radio, may be a little overwhelming. But you can ask an elder to help you as these forms of advertising give better results.

For a start, you can tell people around where you live that you would love to clean their houses for a fee. You can also ask your friends and family to pass the message to their friends. For even better results, make fliers and give them to people you know.

And when you get a few clients, you must offer them a discount if they refer you to their friends. This will grow your customer base and enable you to make more money.

However, I would recommend that you only work for people you know. Getting associated with strangers is not safe. And you must always tell your parents of where you are working every time. Your safety should come first.

## How Much Can You Make?

It's such a simple question, but one with a difficult answer. Actually, the answer is not difficult – it's just that it is not as specific as you would want it to be.

The amount of money you can make in this business varies. Reasons for this include:

- your location

- experience

- the number of hours you are willing to work

- and your price per hour.

But for general purposes, prices range from $3 - $15 per hour. To get a definite answer, find people who clean houses in your area, and ask them how much they make.

# Chapter 2: Grow and Sell Vegetables

Food is an important part of our lives. It's one of the things that fuels our existence. Since you are just a kid, I wouldn't suggest that you open a farm – managing one is no walk in the park. But something you would pull off is the growing of vegetables around your house. There is probably some space lying around you can use to make money.

## Why Should You Grow Vegetables

There are a couple of things that would inspire you to grow vegetables. Here are some of them:

*You will provide customers with fresh veggies* – the majority of vegetables in stores are far from fresh. They usually travel long distances before they get on the shelves. And the longer they stay there, the less nutritious they have.

*Control what goes into the veggies* – with store-bought vegetables, you have no control of what chemicals are used. And these could be dangerous to your health. If you start growing veggies, you can decide to stay away from chemicals.

*Nice way to exercise* – current lifestyles make it impossible to get enough physical activity. But if you start a garden, taking care of your veggies will force you to be on your feet.

## How To Get Started

Establishing a vegetable garden is a lot of work. But the best part is that once it's underway, maintaining it is easy. Here is how you can get started:

*Choose land* – vegetables need food just like you do. So you must ensure that you grow them on a fertile land. But even then, it is important to apply manure for increased fertility.

*Get seeds* – you must buy enough seeds. Since this may be the first time you are growing vegetables, you may need to ask someone who has been doing it on the quantity you need. You must get seeds of different varieties of vegetables.

*Get manure* – artificial manure can drift into water sources and pollute it. It also destroys the very soil you are trying to enrich in the long run. As an alternative, you must go for organic manures.

*Choose natural pesticides* – again, you must avoid artificial pesticides as they also have negative effects on the environment. If you have to use pesticides, choose those from natural sources.

*Keep animals away* – depending on the location of your garden, you may need to fence it. This will keep animals from destroying your vegetables. However, you don't have to buy expensive materials to achieve this. Simple nets should be fine.

## Selling Your Vegetables

Vegetables grow fast. So they should be ready for sale in a few weeks. Below are things you will need to remember when it's time to sell:

*Advertise* – if your garden is located in a place where people can't see it, you will need to advertise that you are selling veggies. Putting a large sign in front of your house works really well. Besides, it's easy and does not cost anything.

*Calculate your profit* – you are growing vegetables to make money. And the only way you will know if you are being successful is to calculate your profits. There are many tools that can be used for this online.

# Chapter 3: Make a Lemonade Stand

Hot weather forces people out of their homes during the summer months. But amidst the fun that comes with the sunny days lies dehydration. As a kid trying to make money, you've got a job of quenching people's thirst.

Many don't like the taste of plain water, which makes lemonade a great option. If you can locate your stand in an area with a lot of people, you can make some good money.

**Things You Will Need**

The best part is that you don't need a lot of things to make a lemonade stand. And the majority of tools to get started may be available in your house. Here is a list of some of the things you need:

*Table* – this must be stable and big enough to accommodate your tools.

*Sign* – again, there is no need to spend money on this. A piece of paper is enough to let people know that you are selling lemonade.

*Bag or tin* – once you start getting a lot of customers, your pockets may fail to contain the money getting into them. This is the reason a bag or a tin is necessary. Just make sure that you put it somewhere secure.

*Chair* – sitting for too long is bad for your healthy, so I encourage you to stand most of the times. Besides, you will not serve anyone while seated. However, you may still need a chair to use when you get tired.

*Trashcan* – we all have the responsibility of taking care of the environment. So a trash can is necessary to keep your stand tidy.

*Lemonade ingredients* – depending on the type of lemonade you want to make, the list of ingredients may vary. But for general purposes, sugar, ice, lemons, and water are the basics.


**Tips for Success**

Opening a lemonade stand can be intimidating if it's your first time. But when you get over that first hurdle, another issue is the responsibility of running your business. Here are some things to keep in mind if you want to be successful:

*Choose a good location* – in business, location is everything. You should plant your lemonade stand in an area with a lot of people. A park, a beach, a church, or outside a grocery store are some good locations you can think of. But before settling anywhere, get permission from the owner.

*Make your sign attractive* – think of your sign as an advertisement. The more attractive it is, the more people it will call. So you must do your best to make it spectacular. There are no hard rules on how you can do this - so get creative. Drawing some lemons on it is not such a bad idea. Just don't forget to include the price of your lemonade.

*Hygiene matters* – first impressions count. People will judge your lemonade before they drink it based on how smart you look. So make sure that you are clean. The same goes for you stand. If you have long hair, you must tie it back.

*Be friendly* – you must also ensure that you are nice to your customers. The importance of this cannot be overstated. Smiling at people when they get to your stand is a good start.

*Sell other things* – to maximize your profits, you can also sell other things you know people may need on a hot day. This may include water and snacks.

*Learn to calculate profit* – before you spend your money on anything, you must be clear of how much money you have in your pocket. And when you start spending, you must keep track of your expenditure. You will use this to calculate how much you have lost and how much you have earned. This is how you will know if you are making profits.

# Chapter 4: Make Money Playing Games

Many kids spend hours every day playing video games. And they do this for fun. But did you know that you can make money with these games? If you think that's a crazy idea of earning money, then you are not alone. The majority of those who come across this idea think the same.

Unfortunately, making money with video games is not as fun as it sounds. Actually, it is so much like any job. It can get boring sometimes.

**Ways of Making Money with Games**

There are a couple of ways you can follow to make money with video games. Here are some of them:

*Take part in esport tournaments* – want to go down in history as someone who made an insane amount of money playing games? Then take part in esport tournaments. But there is one problem – it's only the best of the best that make it at such tournaments. So if you want to get to the top, you must work for it.

*Test games* – this is among the most popular ways of making money with video games. As a game tester, you detect bugs in new games. It can be fun in that you get to play games before anyone else. Unfortunately, since this is a job, you may be forced to play games you don't enjoy. At the same time, the pay tends to be on the lower side. So to make a substantial amount, you may need to work hard.

*Make guides* – if you are good at playing certain games, you can teach others your skill. Your guides can be in videos or in form of blog posts. If you are making posts, you will have to monetize your website. If you are making videos and uploading them to YouTube, you will also find ways of monetizing your channel. But this strategy requires is a lot of work, especially in the beginning. If your content is good, success may come quicker than you think.

*Write reviews* – all you have to do is create a website where you can write game reviews. You will need to monetize the website by placing ads, selling affiliate products, etc. If creating a website is not an option, you can join an already established website and make game reviews for it. You would then be paid for each post you make.

**Tips for Success**

As with everything, making money with video games is not easy. But hard work will get you the results you want. Here are some things to keep in mind:

***Stay up to date*** – the last thing you want is to be the last one to know where the game industry is going. Thanks to tech, you can easily keep up with things that matter to you. The internet provides unlimited access to news and everything going on in the industry. Even better, mobile devices are everywhere making it easy to get what you want anywhere.

***Play a lot of games*** – this will keep your skills sharp and will also perfect your weak areas.

***Don't forget to network*** – knowing the influencers in the game industry is a guaranteed way to succeed.

# Chapter 5: Take Care of Pets

Do you love pets? Then perhaps, a job in the pet industry may prove to be fun.

Most pet owners are too busy to take care of their pets. But little Fido needs to be looked after as well. This may be in form of cleaning up, getting physical activity, going to the veterinarian, and a whole lot of other things. If you have the time and willingness, you can do some of these activities for busy pet owners.

The pet industry is growing every year. You can join those who are making money from this billion dollar industry.

**What Jobs Can You Do**

There are a lot of things you can do in this industry. Here are some of the examples:

*Pet walks* – pets also need some physical activity. Unfortunately, their owners may be preoccupied with work and other tasks. This is where you come in. All you need is to take the pet for a walk. And if you feel like, you can walk pets from many clients at once, so more money for you.

*Pet washing* – animals can get stinky without proper cleaning. So some pet owners may hire you to give their animals baths.

*Take dogs to appointments* – you may also be hired to take dogs to check-ups.

*Pet sitting* – these are among the most featured jobs in the pet industry. And it's simple in that you just have to watch the pet when the owner is not around. And it also includes giving their pet food and water. In some areas, the rate can be as high as $100.

**How to Get Started**

Getting your foot in the pet industry is easy. And you don't need to spend much as the most important thing you need is to advertise yourself. Although you will face competition, it is not much as in other industries. And the fact that taking care of pets is a growing business, getting your slice of the pie should not be that hard.

*Do your research first* – just because the pet industry is growing, it doesn't mean it's a hot business in your area. So some research is important. It will give you an idea of the demand for pet caring services where you live. Additionally, you will know the rates that others are charging. You don't want your rates to be too high and you also don't want them to be too low.

***Join a professional organization*** – being a member of an organization like the National Association of Professional Pet Sitters or Professional United Pet Sitters will make getting work easier. It shows clients that you are serious with what you do. Additionally, your membership may give you other perks like higher rates and lessons on how to take care of pets.

***Advertise your business*** – no one will guess that you now work in the pet industry. So to get discovered, you must sell yourself. You can do this by making business cards, telling people through word of mouth, or making fliers. Also, you can create a website.

***Start small*** – you do not need to shoot for the stars from the start; baby steps were made for a reason. If you have a pet at home, you may perfect your skills with it. Ask your parents to pay you so you can take care of it. You can also provide pet caring services to your family and friends.

***Get toys*** – to make your work easier, you must get some toys. Animals like to play.

# Chapter 6: Teach Your Skills

Everyone is good at something. Think about it - what do people usually ask you to help them with? It could be getting around the internet, dealing with a troubled phone, or anything. To you, this may seem like nothing. But to the people you help, it may be worth paying for.

Examples of things you can teach:

*Playing piano* – if you are really good with the piano, you may need to think about making money from your skill and not just doing it for fun. There are a lot of people ready to pay if you could share your passion with them. Although you may argue that anyone can learn a piano from a book, personal touch is important (something you cannot get in a book).

*Teach mathematics* – it may also be that you are good with numbers. Since there are others struggling with math, teaching this subject is another thing you can do.

*Teach dancing* – think you got the moves? Then own the floor and show others how it's done.

*Playing chess* – learning to play chess is easy. But mastering it takes time. And those looking for a quick way to the top may pay you to teach them your secrets.

*Cooking* – you can as well get paid for teaching people how to cook. This can range from baking cakes, making ice cream, baking bread, and much more.

**Tips for Success**

To avoid taking too long before you start making money, you must be smart in the way you do business. Here are some of the ways you can use to achieve that:

*Advertise* – this isn't just about putting ads in the newspaper or on radio. Even telling your friends that you are teaching something should get you going.

*Be friendly* – your customers should enjoy working with you. You must try to be friendly all the time. Smiling is a simple way to do this. And when angry, you must control yourself. If you fail to do this, you will end up driving your customers away.

*Clients must be happy* – every time you finish teaching someone, you must determine if he is happy with the lesson. If you find that he isn't, you must do what you can to make him happy. Satisfied customers are key to the survival of your business. They may refer their friends to you.

*Upgrade your skills* – even when you believe that you are good, you must keep on upgrading your skills. This will keep you relevant to your customers.

*Charge fairly* – you do not want to make your customers feel like they are overpaying for your services. At the same time, you must not feel like you are working for peanuts. What you want is a fair price for both of you. Unfortunately, it is not easy to say how much you should charge. What you are teaching will determine your rate. So do your research first.

# Chapter 7: Wash Cars

The influx of cars has proved to be a burden on the environment. But every story has two sides. Lots of cars provide an opportunity to you to wash cars for busy drivers. And depending on how hard you work, you can make a lot of money in this business.

Unlike other jobs, you do not need extensive experience to start washing cars. And you also do not need to make a huge investment to get operations underway. Actually, you can go from being broke to making money in one week.

**Things You Will Need**

Here is a list of things you will need:

*Good location* – this is the most important thing if you are serious about making money washing cars. A good location will make it easy for customers to find you. Also, you will not spend a lot advertising, the money you save will increase your profits. Ideally, you should locate your car wash along a busy road. Most places near fuel stations prove to be good options. However, you will need to get permission before you start washing cars on somebody's place.

*Water source* – washing cars needs water - a lot of it. So it must be easily accessible. If it is not, you may have to keep your clients waiting as you go to fetch it. And this will hurt your business.

*Cleaning stuff* – this includes sponges, soap, towels, etc. Although you do not need to spend money on expensive cleaning tools, buying them will make your work professional. And this may help attract more customers.


But a good location with a good water source and some cleaning tools are not enough. You must have a sign that tells people that you wash cars. Many write the words "car wash" on a board. However, this should not limit your imagination. Think outside the box and make your sign attractive.


**Pricing**

Your price should be in proportion with the effort that goes into washing a car. At the same time, other expenses must also be taken into consideration. This may include the cost of water and cleaning materials. To ensure that you charging fairly, you must ask other car washers in your area about the prices they charge.

A lower price will drive more cars to your car wash. And this may make you a lot of money. However, in some situations, you may not wash enough cars to even cover your costs. In this case, your low price will lead to losses.

If you decided to charge higher than other car washers, you may not get a lot of customers. But the few you will get may be able to make you a lot of money.

For simplicity, you should charge what everyone else is charging. But before you do, make sure you establish your costs. If this is over your head, consult an adult.

**Should You Partner With a Friend?**

Washing a car is time-consuming. When getting started, you will be able to keep up with the number of cars. But with time, as your business grows, your two hands may not be enough. This will raise the need for you to get a partner. Here is how a partner can help you:

*You will expand your business* – nobody likes to wait, especially when it's something he is paying for. When washing all cars by yourself, customers may have to wait as you wash other cars. And you may lose some of them because of this. But when you have a partner, you will be able to wash a lot of cars in less time.

*Business will go on in your absence* – your partner will run business on days when you are sick or just absent. Consistency is important for success. It makes customers know that they can depend on you.

*Share the burden of running a business* – running a business can be stressful. But when you have a partner, you share the weight. This gives you time to do other important things in your life.

However, partnerships mean sharing everything including the money. If you are okay with this, then you should have no problem.

# Chapter 8: Make a Website

We now have more websites on the internet than ever before. And the number continues to rise as new websites are created daily. Unlike in the past, having no website now is a choice. The cost of domain names, as well as hosting, has come down. And if you want, you can have a functional website for free.

Since you are reading this book to make money, a website is something you should seriously consider. Unfortunately, it doesn't make money as quickly as the other money making methods in this book. But it is sustainable once you get your first pay.

**How To Make Money With a Website**

There are a couple of ways you can use to make money with a website. But in this chapter, I will only focus on the most popular three:

### Sell Affiliate Products

The best part with this is that you do not need to make your own products. Your job is to create a website, fill it with good content, and then promote other people's products on it. You then receive a commission for every sale made.

Some popular websites with affiliate programs include Amazon, ShareASale, Clickbank, and others.

### Put Ads on Your Website

Another easy way is to put advertisements on your website. Every time a reader clicks these ads, you get paid. Just as with affiliate marketing, you also need good content on your website. This will attract a lot of people and increase the number of ads clicked.

### Make Your Own Products

The problem with the two methods above is that you only get a small percentage of the money made. So if you want to eat the whole cake alone, making your own products and selling them on your website is the way to go. The products can be books, software, or just about anything you can think of.

### How to Create a Website

Creating a website is easy these days. The only skill you need is knowing how to get around the internet. There are scripts that will guide you through the whole process of making the website. And if you get stuck, there are a lot of tutorials you can use.

However, there are some important things you must keep in mind. Here they are:

*Choose a good name* – the name of your website must be memorable. It must also represent what your website is all about. And still, it must remain short. Although you can get a free domain name, I would recommend that you buy one. A name like www.yoursite.com looks more professional than www.wordpress.yoursite.com.

*Pick a good host* – you must also try to avoid free hosting. Remember, there is no such thing as a free lunch.

**Tips for Getting More Traffic**

Making money with a website requires that you have one thing – traffic. Without this, your work will be seen by no one, which means no money in your account.

Here are some tips you should use to increase traffic:

*Write great content* – if this was 10 or 15 years ago, you could fill your website with mediocre content and still rank highly in search results. But search engines are now smarter. So you must take time to make content that will be useful to your readers.

*Focus on SEO* – this means making your website attractive to search engines. However, SEO is a huge topic, and you cannot master it in a day. I would recommend that you get a book to learn more about it. Additionally, you can subscribe to one of the many SEO blogs on the internet.

***Do Guest Blogging*** – by guest blogging, you will be getting backlinks. These are links on other websites that point to your website and act like votes. Having a lot of these will get you a lot of love from search engines.

***Don't Forget Social Media*** – apart from search engines, social media sites are another good source of traffic. So make sure that you know the social networking sites your audience hangs on and focus on them.

However, if you are not 18, there is not much you can do on the internet on your own. In this case, you will have to involve your parents.

# Conclusion

I'm sure you now know what you can do to make money. Not only will this make you become independent, buts it's also a good way to earn extra money to buy things you need.

With all the money-making methods in the book, you may be tempted to try everything. But that is a recipe for failure. You will get overwhelmed and you will quit before you achieve your goal. Instead, you must choose one or two methods to focus on. This will allow you to become an expert in that method of making money.

Another thing you shouldn't forget is to keep upgrading your knowledge. Learning is important in that it gives you new skills. It also improves your weak spots.

But learning doesn't always mean spending thousands of dollars to get into a classroom. You can learn things from people who have been doing what you want to do. You may also learn a thing or two from the internet.

My last advice is that you should keep on working hard. The importance of this point cannot be overstated. Your job may get boring. So you should be dedicated to what you want to achieve in the end.

# About the Author

Dr. Usman is an MD, now pursuing his post-graduation degree. As a medical doctor, he has deep insight in all aspects of health, fitness and nutrition.

He is a certified nutritionist and a personal trainer. With these qualifications, he has helped countless people reach their health, fitness and weight loss goals.

Dr. Usman is an avid researcher with 20+ publications in internationally accepted peer reviewed journals.

He is an accomplished writer with more than 5 years of writing experience. In this time, he has produced countless blogs, articles and research work on topics related to health, fitness and nutrition.

He is a published author with more than 100+ books published and several more in the pipe line.

Finally, he runs his own blog and posts health, fitness and nutrition related articles there regularly. You can visit his blog at http://hcures.com/.

Check out some of the other JD-Biz Publishing books

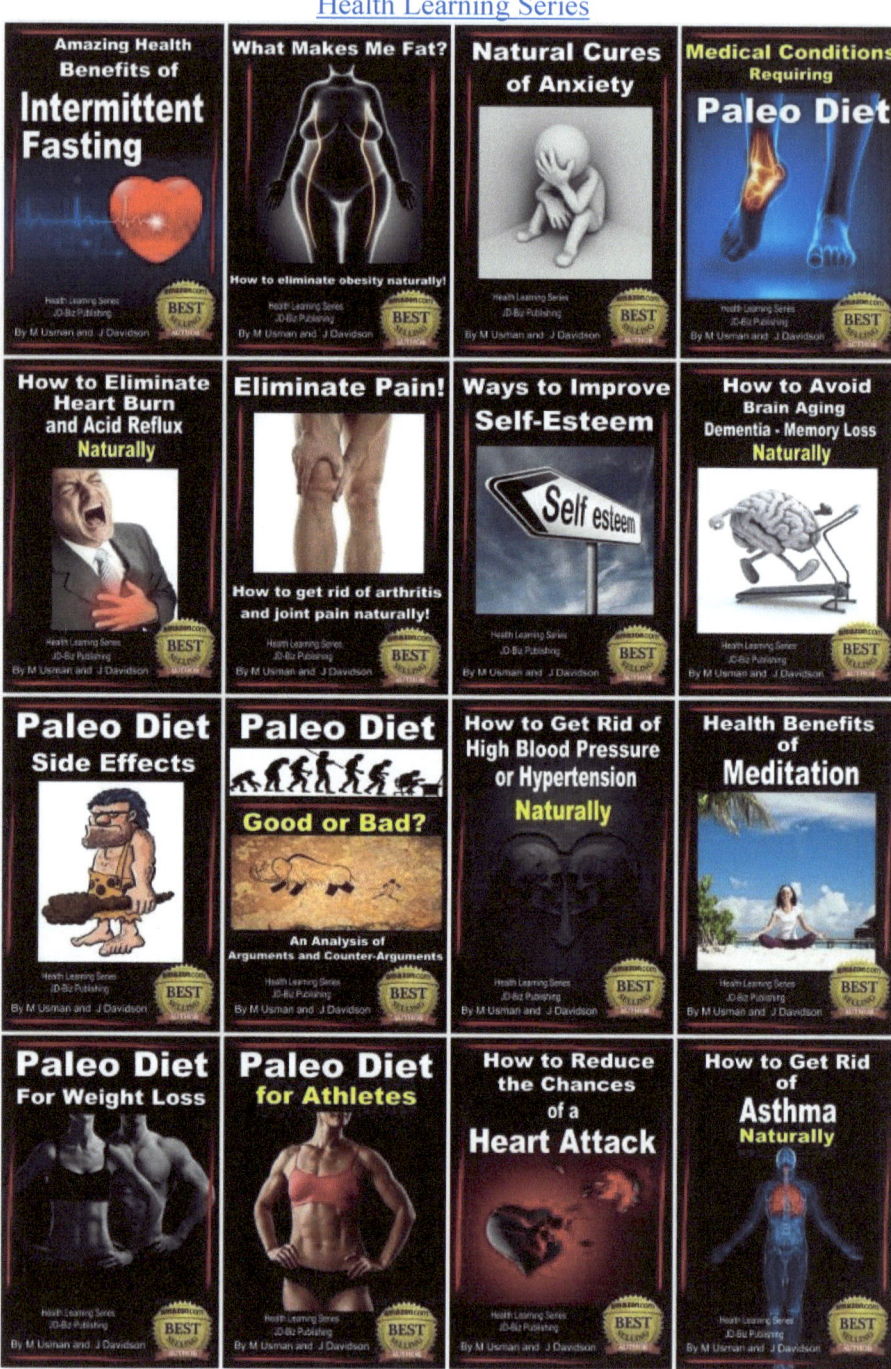

# Amazing Animal Book Series

## Our books are available at

1. Amazon.com

2. Barnes and Noble

3. Itunes

4. Kobo

5. Smashwords

6. Google Play Books


**Download Free Books!**
**http://MendonCottageBooks.com**

# Publisher

JD-Biz Corp

P O Box 374

Mendon, Utah 84325

http://www.jd-biz.com/

Mendon Cottage Books

P O Box 374, Mendon Utah 84325

www.ingramcontent.com/pod-product-compliance
Lightning Source LLC
Chambersburg PA
CBHW041113180526
45172CB00001B/227